APR 7 2004

W9-CEI-372

Landmark
Events in
American
History

# The Bombing of
# Pearl Harbor

Michael V. Uschan

**WORLD ALMANAC® LIBRARY**

*To Gaël Mustapha*

Please visit our web site at: www.worldalmanaclibrary.com
For a free color catalog describing World Almanac® Library's list of high-quality books and multimedia programs, call 1-800-848-2928 (USA) or 1-800-387-3178 (Canada). World Almanac® Library's fax: (414) 332-3567.

**Library of Congress Cataloging-in-Publication Data**

Uschan, Michael V., 1948-
      The bombing of Pearl Harbor / by Michael V. Uschan.
          p. cm. — (Landmark events in American history)
      Includes bibliographical references and index.
      ISBN 0-8368-5373-3 (lib. bdg.)
      ISBN 0-8368-5401-2 (softcover)
      1.  Pearl Harbor (Hawaii), Attack on, 1941—Juvenile literature.   2.  United States—Foreign relations—Japan—Juvenile literature.   3.  Japan—Foreign relations—United States—Juvenile literature.   4.  World War, 1939-1945—Causes—Juvenile literature.   [1.  Pearl Harbor (Hawaii), Attack on, 1941.
      2.  World War, 1939-1945—Causes.]   I. Title.   II. Series.
      D767.92.U8    2003
      940.54'26—dc21                                                              2002036022

First published in 2003 by
**World Almanac® Library**
330 West Olive Street, Suite 100
Milwaukee, WI  53212  USA

Copyright © 2003 by World Almanac® Library.

Produced by Discovery Books
Editor: Sabrina Crewe
Designer and page production: Sabine Beaupré
Photo researcher: Sabrina Crewe
Maps and diagrams: Stefan Chabluk
World Almanac® Library editorial driection: Mark J. Sachner
World Almanac® Library art direction: Tammy Gruenewald
World Almanac® Library production: Jessica Yanke

Photo credits: Corbis: cover, pp. 6, 7, 8, 10, 11, 12, 13, 15, 18, 19, 21, 24, 26, 28 (both), 30, 31, 32, 33, 34, 35, 37, 38, 39, 40, 41; USS *Arizona* Memorial, National Park Service, Photo Collection: pp. 4, 5, 16, 17, 20, 22, 23, 25, 27, 29, 42, 43.

Printed in the United States of America

1 2 3 4 5 6 7 8 9 07 06 05 04 03

# Contents

# Introduction

## War Around the World

By December 1941, World War II had been raging for some years. Japan had invaded China in 1937, starting the fighting in Asia. In September 1939, Germany brought war to Europe when it attacked and defeated neighboring Poland. Millions of people—soldiers and **civilians**—were killed during the course of World War II. Until 1941, however, Americans had been divided over whether they should help defend their **allies** in a war that had already engulfed the rest of the world.

## Attack on the United States

All this changed on December 7, 1941, when the United States itself was attacked. The surprise aerial assault by Japan was aimed at Oahu, one of the Hawaiian islands in the Pacific Ocean lying 2,400 miles (3,860 kilometers) west of San Francisco. In 1941, Hawaii was a **United States Territory**, and the headquarters of the

U.S. Navy in the Pacific were at Pearl Harbor on Oahu. The Japanese planes that day killed 2,388 Americans, 68 of them civilians, and wounded 1,178 sailors, soldiers, and civilians. The attack destroyed or damaged dozens of ships and hundred of planes at nearby U.S. military bases.

## Entry into World War II

The rain of deadly bombs and bullets did much more than shatter the peace of a calm, sunny Sunday morning with death and destruction. The shocking attack by a nation that had not declared war against the United States horrified and angered Americans. It galvanized them into entering World War II, a conflict many Americans had not wanted to join because they had not believed it directly affected them.

The day after Japanese planes bombed Pearl Harbor, President Franklin D. Roosevelt predicted December 7, 1941, would be "a date which will live in **infamy**." And it has. The surprise attack on U.S. Navy ships anchored in Pearl Harbor in Hawaii is still remembered as one of the most tragic days in U.S. history.

The attack made Americans realize they could not ignore what was happening in the rest of the world. It shattered forever the belief that the Pacific and Atlantic Oceans protected them from other countries. It also made Americans determined to defend their country and to avenge the men and women who died that terrible day.

**A Date Which Will Live in Infamy**
"Yesterday, December 7, 1941—a date which will live in infamy—the United States of America was suddenly and deliberately attacked by naval and air forces of the Empire of Japan. . . . No matter how long it may take us to overcome this premeditated invasion, the American people in their righteous might will win through to absolute victory."

*President Franklin D. Roosevelt, December 8, 1941, in a speech asking Congress to declare war on Japan*

On December 8, 1941, President Franklin D. Roosevelt delivered a war message to Congress. The U.S. government then declared war on Japan.

# Chapter 1

# World War II

Adolf Hitler, the fascist leader of Germany, stands with other Nazis at a Nazi Party rally. Hitler was responsible for the death of millions of people during World War II.

### Germany After World War I

The social and political factors that caused World War II grew out of the bitter peace following World War I. In that war—which lasted from 1914 to 1918—Britain, France, and other nations including the United States had defeated Germany. The Treaty of Versailles in 1919 forced Germany to pay the Allies millions of dollars in war damages. It also took away some European territory that Germany controlled. The treaty terms destroyed Germany's **economy** and made Germans bitter toward their conquerors.

In the 1920s, a new and popular political leader named Adolf Hitler emerged in Germany. Hitler was a fascist, someone who believed government should wield supreme power over its citizens. He told Germans that they should be proud of their nation and promised to make Germany strong again. Hitler headed the National Socialist (Nazi) Party. In January 1933, Hitler's party had grown so strong that he was elected chancellor, Germany's most powerful official. Within a few months, Hitler abolished Germany's **democratic** laws and became a dictator.

## Fascism

Fascism is a political system in which the government has complete authority over its citizens. Power is usually wielded by one leader, and any opposition is crushed. Fascists believe that their nation and race are superior to all others. To Hitler, Jews belonged to another race, and it was his intention to wipe them out in Europe.

The word *fascism* was first used in 1919 by Italian fascist leader Benito Mussolini. The Italian word is derived from the Latin word *fasces*, which refers to a bundle of rods with an ax in it, a symbol of the supreme authority of the state.

### Hitler Goes to War

Hitler believed that to become strong again, Germany needed to gain new territory. He began this quest by building up Germany's armed forces in defiance of the Versailles Treaty, which had decreed that the defeated nation could not have a strong military force. In 1938, after Germany had grown strong enough, Hitler seized neighboring Austria, the country of his birth. That same year, Hitler's army invaded and took control of the Sudetenland, a region of Czechoslovakia where many German-speaking people lived. In March 1939, his army occupied the rest of Czechoslovakia.

It seemed nothing could stop Hitler's forces and—at first—other countries, such as Britain and the United States, did nothing in response. On September 1, 1939, however, when Hitler invaded Poland, the Allies decided to fight. Britain and France declared war on Germany, and World War II began in Europe.

In June 1940, German troops entered the French capital of Paris, and France was under German occupation. These German motorcycle troops are parading down one of the main streets of Paris.

## Italy and Japan

Italy was also a fascist nation. During the 1920s, Benito Mussolini had assumed power in Italy in much the same way Hitler would later win control of Germany. Japan was ruled by military leaders who had overturned a more moderate leadership. Like Germany, Italy and Japan also seized other countries to increase their own wealth and power. Italy invaded Ethiopia in 1935 and Albania in 1939, and Japan invaded China in 1937 as the first step in its plan to conquer the entire Far East.

Germany, Italy, and Japan became allies during the course of World War II. They were known as the Axis Powers.

## Isolationists

In September 1940, the Axis Powers signed a pact pledging to help each other if any one of them was attacked by the United States. Most Americans supported the Allies, but they were isolationists. This meant they believed their nation was better off not being involved in the affairs of other nations, especially foreign wars.

In the late 1930s, when Germany and Japan began attacking other nations, isolationists who controlled Congress—such as Senator Burton K. Wheeler of Montana—helped pass several **Neutrality** Acts. These laws prohibited the United States from helping countries threatened by aggression and were intended to keep the nation out of any new wars.

Japanese troops march through the Chungsun Gate that leads to Nanking, capital of China, in the invasion of 1937. Japanese leaders believed their nation should take control of Asia.

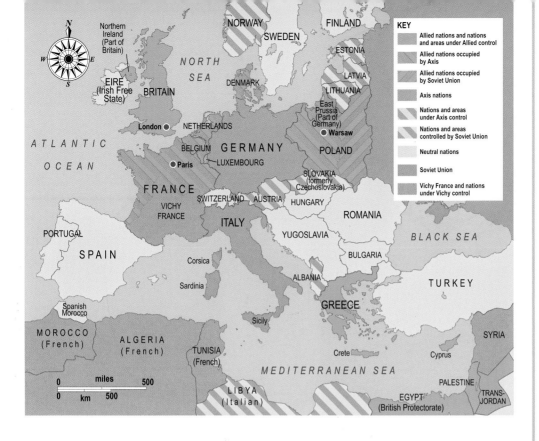

This map shows how Europe and North Africa were divided into Allied, Axis, and neutral nations in 1940. In addition to the nations shown here, Canada had joined the Allies, but the United States was still a neutral nation.

## FDR's Presidency

When Democrat Franklin D. Roosevelt was elected president in 1932, the United States was in the grip of the Great Depression, the worst economic downturn in U.S. history. Roosevelt eased the suffering of Americans with huge new government programs that created jobs and distributed food and financial aid to needy citizens.

## An Isolationist Nation

The United States had usually refused to ally itself with other countries because it feared becoming involved in their wars. George Washington, the nation's first president, advised Americans, "Tis your true **policy** to steer clear of permanent Alliances, with any portion of the foreign World." Thomas Jefferson, the third U.S. president, also warned the United States against "entangling alliances" with foreign countries.

The United States temporarily abandoned its isolationist stance in 1917 to help defeat Germany in World War I. But after the war was over, the United States retreated again from its involvement with the affairs of other countries.

President Roosevelt made regular radio broadcasts to the nation during his presidency. These were known as "fireside chats."

When Roosevelt was elected for a second term in 1936, he began focusing on foreign affairs. Isolationists still controlled U.S. foreign policy, but Roosevelt was an **interventionist**. He tried to convince his country that the United States needed to help nations being attacked by the Axis Powers. Roosevelt feared that if the United States did nothing, those countries would conquer large parts of the world and the United States would become "a lone island in a world dominated by the philosophy of force."

## Franklin Delano Roosevelt (1882—1945)

Franklin Delano Roosevelt, the nation's thirty-second president, was born at Hyde Park, New York, into a wealthy and powerful family. His distant cousin, Theodore, had also been president. In 1921, when Franklin D. Roosevelt was thirty-nine years old, he was stricken with polio. He soon needed crutches to walk and, as he grew older, was confined to a wheelchair. Despite this physical problem, Roosevelt served as governor of New York and was elected president in 1932. He was the only president ever elected for more than two terms. He served longer than any other chief executive, from March 4, 1933, until his death on April 12, 1945. Roosevelt is considered one of the greatest, most important presidents in U.S. history. He helped the United States survive the Great Depression of the 1920s and 1930s and helped the Allies to the brink of victory over Japan and Germany in World War II. Roosevelt died just before the end of the war.

At first, isolationists kept Roosevelt from acting to help other nations. But in the spring of 1940—when Germany overpowered France and was threatening Britain—isolationist feeling weakened as Americans began to fear what was happening. In the summer and fall of 1940, Roosevelt persuaded Congress to give billions of dollars to strengthen the U.S. military. He also got Congress to establish the first peacetime military **draft** in U.S. history.

## The Lend-Lease Plan

In December 1940, Roosevelt proposed the Lend-**Lease** Plan. He wanted the United States to loan ships, planes, and weapons to Britain so it could continue fighting Germany. In exchange, Britain would lease some British territory to the United States. The plan passed in early 1941 over the opposition of Senator Wheeler, who claimed it would lead to a war that could "plow under every fourth American boy."

The United States was strengthening its military so it could protect itself if it was attacked. But Americans were still not ready to go to war themselves to stop Germany and Japan.

**A Sense of Urgency**
"We must be the great arsenal of democracy. For us this is an emergency as serious as war itself. We must apply ourselves to our task with the same resolution, the same sense of urgency, the same spirit of patriotism and sacrifice as we would show were we at war."

*President Franklin D. Roosevelt, December 29, 1940, making an argument for the Lend-Lease Plan*

Workers at this factory in Akron, Ohio, assemble antiaircraft guns for use during World War II. Before the war, the plant had been a tire factory.

# The United States in the Pacific

Hawaiian Queen Lili'uokalani was the last monarch to rule Hawaii. Her government was overthrown by Americans in January 1893.

Most U.S. citizens were opposed to their nation making alliances with other nations, but they did not want the United States to be completely isolated from the rest of the world. They wanted to do business with other countries so their country could become richer. They also wanted the United States to protect its economic interests overseas.

## A U.S. Territory

It was for both of these reasons that the United States came to possess Hawaii. This cluster of eight islands in the Pacific Ocean had ports that were important stopping places for U.S. ships traveling to the Far East to trade with China and other countries in the region.

Hawaii was traditionally ruled by members of Hawaiian royalty. In 1891, Hawaiian monarch King Kalakaua died and was succeeded by Queen Lili'uokalani. She was the last monarch to rule Hawaii as an independent kingdom.

By the 1890s, many American businessmen in Hawaii were becoming wealthy from the sugar industry. They wanted Hawaii to become a U.S. possession because they did not want to share its wealth with other countries.

On January 16, 1893, a group of American residents used force to overthrow the government of Queen Lili'uokalani. Although the takeover was illegal, the businessmen who led the revolt established what they called the Republic of Hawaii. On July 7, 1898, President William McKinley signed a bill to **annex** Hawaii, and two years later it became a U.S. Territory. Distant Hawaii was now part of the United States.

## Japanese Aggression

In the late nineteenth and early twentieth century, the United States had developed important economic and political ties with countries in the Far East such as China. It was because of those interests that the United States became increasingly concerned in the 1930s about Japanese aggression in the Pacific.

In 1931, Japan invaded Manchuria, a northern region of China. U.S. officials protested the illegal move but did nothing else. In 1937, Japan launched a second invasion of China, a military attack that many historians claim marked the beginning of World War II.

Sugarcane fields stretch across the Hawaiian landscape. The United States annexed Hawaii in 1898 because of American interest in Hawaii's sugar and other **assets**.

**The Ripe Pear**

"The Hawaiian pear is now fully ripe and this is the golden hour for the United States to pluck it."

*John L. Stevens, U.S. Minister to Hawaii, writing to his superiors in Washington, D.C., in the early 1890s*

13

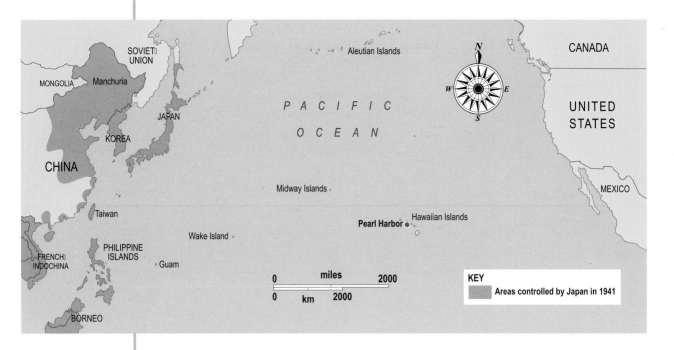

This map shows where the Hawaiian Islands are in the Pacific Ocean. The pink areas were controlled by Japan in 1941.

## The U.S. Response

President Roosevelt condemned Japan's actions. Ignoring the Neutrality Acts, he began sending arms and aid to China so it could defend itself. In May 1940, fearing other attacks by Japan in the Far East, Roosevelt transferred the headquarters for the U.S. Navy's Pacific **Fleet** from California to Hawaii. Pearl Harbor's position now became very important. Lying midway between the United States and the Far East, Pearl Harbor was a possible launching point for military action against Japan.

When the United States continued to oppose Japan's aggression, Japan came to believe it would have to fight back. From the Japanese point of view, the United States was not neutral, and it was threatening Japan. Admiral Isoroku Yamamoto of the Japanese navy was especially worried about the U.S. ships stationed in Pearl Harbor, which he considered "a dagger being pointed at our throat."

### The Epidemic of War

"The epidemic of world lawlessness is spreading. War is a contagion, whether it is declared or undeclared. There is no escape through mere isolation or neutrality. There must be positive endeavors to preserve peace."

*President Franklin D. Roosevelt, October 5, 1937, condemning Japan's invasion of China*

# Pearl Harbor

Pearl Harbor took its name from the many oysters that Hawaiians harvested from its waters. The Hawaiians originally called the area Wai Momi, which in English means "pearl waters." Pearl Harbor is a protected harbor six miles (10 km) west of the city of Honolulu. The United States obtained exclusive rights to the harbor in 1887, even before Hawaii was annexed, and it was used as a place to repair and refuel ships. By 1911, the harbor had been deepened so the largest naval ships could enter it. It has 10 square miles (26 square kilometers) of **navigable** water. It has three distinct areas named East Loch, Middle Loch, and West Loch. Pearl Harbor Naval Station also comprises 10,000 acres (4,000 hectares) of land. This includes Ford Island, located at the lower end of East Loch. The island boasts military facilities, including an air base. Surrounding the harbor, the navy has constructed buildings to house supplies, training centers, offices, a hospital, and a navy yard to repair ships.

Pearl Harbor today, with Ford Island visible (center right) beyond the mainland.

Admiral Isoroku Yamamoto was commander in chief of the Imperial Navy of Japan. He was killed in 1943 during the war in the Pacific.

## Heading Toward War

In July 1941, Japan invaded French Indochina and seemed ready to attack other countries, such as the Philippines. The Philippines had been governed by the United States since the Spanish-American War in 1898.

President Roosevelt responded by freezing Japanese assets in the United States and refusing to sell it any more oil, steel, or other war supplies. Japan needed those products to keep fighting, especially the oil that fueled its ships, planes, and tanks. Japan, therefore, considered the U.S. decision a hostile one.

In October, General Hideki Tojo became Japan's prime minister. He decided to fight the United States. Tojo's first step toward war was to approve a daring plan Admiral Yamamoto had devised to cripple the Pacific Fleet by attacking Pearl Harbor with planes launched from aircraft carriers.

To be successful, the attack had to be a surprise. In an attempt to disguise its war-like intentions, Japan began a new round of peace talks with the United States in November 1941.

## A Warning of War

The negotiations were only meant to lull the United States into a false sense of security. This was something that U.S. officials soon learned because of something they called "Magic." The Japanese sent messages to **diplomats** overseas in a secret code known as "Purple." Unknown to Japan, U.S. **intelligence** officials had developed a machine—nicknamed Magic—that allowed them to decode and read the messages.

In November, U.S. officials intercepted messages that indicated Japan would reject U.S. demands that it must pull out of China and

Lieutenant General Walter Short (left) and Admiral Husband Kimmel (right) were the commanders at Pearl Harbor when it was attacked in December 1941. They are seen here with British Admiral Louis Mountbatten (center).

Indochina. U.S. officials now knew the continuing negotiations were not being conducted in good faith. They also began to suspect that, when the talks did end, Japan might declare war on the United States.

Because of this, on November 27, officials in Washington issued a "war warning" to U.S. Pacific bases. The message said negotiations with the Japanese were going badly. In Hawaii, the warnings went to Admiral Husband E. Kimmel, commander of the Pacific Fleet, and Lieutenant General Walter Short, who commanded ground forces there.

Although U.S. officials feared the Japanese might attack U.S. forces when the talks ended, they believed the strike would come in the Philippines or some other spot in the Far East. They did not believe Japan would strike Pearl Harbor, even though the possibility had been discussed. This created a false sense of security that led both Kimmel and Short to feel that their bases were safe.

**Expecting Aggression**

"This dispatch is to be considered a war warning: Negotiations with Japan have ceased and an aggressive move by Japan is expected within the next few days. Japanese troops and naval task forces indicate an **amphibious** expedition against either the Philippines, Thailand . . . or possibly Borneo. Execute an appropriate defensive **deployment**."

*Admiral Harold R. Stark, part of the war warning issued November 27, 1941*

## December 7, 1941

The warning went out on November 27, but U.S. officials were still waiting for the top Japanese diplomats in Washington, D.C.—Kichisaburo Nomura and Saburo Kurusu—to deliver Japan's final response to their demands. On December 6, Japan began sending its response to its diplomats in Washington in a fourteen-part message. It was immediately intercepted by U.S. intelligence officers, who began decoding it.

The long statement indicated Japan would not agree to Roosevelt's demands to end its aggression in China. When Roosevelt was given the message at 9:30 P.M. on December 6, he knew that any chance for peace was dead. "This means war," he told Harry Hopkins, his chief adviser.

On Sunday morning, December 7, intelligence agents decoded a fifteenth part to the message. It directed Nomura and Kurusu to deliver the response to the White House at 1:00 P.M. that day. Realizing that Japan might attack after that time, the War Department issued a new alert to U.S. bases in the Pacific at noon Washington time. The warning mentioned the 1:00 P.M. appointment the Japanese had made to meet with U.S. officials and said,

Japanese Ambassador Kichisaburo Nomura (left) and Japanese special envoy Saburo Kurusu (right) chat with U.S. Secretary of State Cordell Hull (center) after a meeting with the president. In November 1941 these parties were still discussing peace, even as the Japanese carrier force headed toward Pearl Harbor.

"Just what significance the hour set may have, we do not know, but be on the alert accordingly."

The significance of the appointment was the five-hour time difference between Washington and Hawaii. When the diplomatic note was due to be delivered at 1:00 P.M., it would be 8:00 A.M. in Hawaii. And that was the time at which Japanese planes began their attack on Pearl Harbor.

## A Disastrous Delay

The attempt to alert Kimmel and Short to possible danger failed because the warning was not delivered in time. Military leaders did not believe Pearl Harbor would be attacked, and so War Department officials did not bother to contact Kimmel and Short immediately. Instead, the warning message was sent to Kimmel and Short as a regular telegram.

The telegram did not arrive in Honolulu, Hawaii, until 7:33 A.M., a half hour before the attack started. After further delay, the message was given to messenger Tadeo Fuchimaki, who set off on his motorcycle for the U.S. Army headquarters at Fort Shafter to deliver the warning. By the time the rider got there, the attack was over.

A view of the Pearl Harbor naval base as it was in its quiet days before the attack. Two submarines can be seen at the dock.

# Chapter 3

# The Attack on Pearl Harbor

### The Japanese Fleet Arrives

The Japanese ship *Akagi* was one of the thirty-three war ships and support vessels, including six **aircraft carriers**, that had left Japan on November 26, 1941. The attack fleet, commanded by Admiral Chuichi Nagumo, had crossed 4,000 miles (6,400 km) of open sea to a spot 220 miles (350 km) north of Oahu. The Japanese reached the launch point for the strike on Pearl Harbor without being detected by the United States.

### The First Wave

At 6:00 A.M. on December 7, 1941, in the deep dark before dawn, the first wave of 183 Japanese war planes took off from the Japanese

## The Attackers

The Japanese attacked with several types of planes. High-level bombers dropped explosives from several thousand feet in the air. Dive bombers flew low over targets before releasing their bombs. Torpedo planes released torpedoes into the harbor after making low-level runs toward targets; the self-propelled torpedoes then raced through the water until they hit something and exploded.

Two torpedoes destined for Pearl Harbor on the deck of the Japanese aircraft carrier *Akagi*.

Early on December 7, 1941, a group of Japanese pilots and sailors wave as a bomber prepares to depart from the carrier *Zuikaku* to attack Pearl Harbor. A Japanese flag flies on the mast.

ship *Akagi* and began flying toward Pearl Harbor. Thirty minutes later, a second group of 167 planes was launched. Japanese bomber pilot Abe Zenji remembered how the planes looked as they flew away: "It was like the sky was filled with fireflies."

At 7:52 A.M., the first wave of the attack roared over the northern coast of Oahu. Commander Fuchida Mitsuo radioed back to Nagumo, "*Tora! Tora! Tora!*" In Japanese, *tora* means "tiger"—it was the code word that meant the Japanese had surprised their enemy. The signal marked the beginning of the worst day in U.S. naval history.

## Missed Warnings

The attack was a surprise to the 100,000 U.S. soldiers and sailors stationed on Oahu. There were two incidents that took place shortly before the air raid, however, that should have alerted them to the approaching danger.

At 6:45 A.M., the USS *Ward*, while on patrol, fired on and sank a small two-man Japanese submarine in restricted waters off Pearl Harbor. The vessel was one of five midget subs that larger Japanese submarines had released near the harbor entrance the night before.

This picture, taken from a Japanese warplane, shows Ford Island in the opening moments of the attack. After a direct hit, a plume of water spurts up from the battleship *Oklahoma* at anchor in Battleship Row.

Lieutenant William Outerbridge, commanding officer of the *Ward*, radioed a report of the action he had taken to naval headquarters. Officials there, however, dismissed his claim that he had sunk an enemy submarine. Believing it was a false alarm, they instructed Outerbridge to keep investigating.

Just minutes later, at 7:02 A.M., at a **radar** installation on Oahu's north coast, Privates Joseph Lockard and George Elliott noticed blips on their screens. The signal indicated a large group of planes was flying toward Oahu. When the soldiers alerted their duty officer by phone, Lieutenant Kermit Tyler told them, "Don't worry about it." Tyler said the planes showing up on radar were U.S. B-17 bombers due to arrive that morning from California. He was wrong. The planes were Japanese and the attack was about to begin.

## Bombing the Ships

As the first wave of planes reached Pearl Harbor, their pilots saw a sheltered, oddly shaped bay that resembled a piece from a giant jigsaw puzzle. In the center was Ford Island, where the naval air station lay. Next to Ford Island was Battleship Row, where the navy's biggest ships were moored side by side. In all, more than ninety battleships, destroyers, cruisers, and support ships were anchored that day in Pearl Harbor.

The first bombs fell at 7:55 A.M. In just a few minutes, the battleships *West Virginia*, *Oklahoma*, and *California* were all hit and sinking. The battleships were the main target, but smaller vessels were also damaged or destroyed. The **minelayer** *Oglala* was blown apart by the impact of the bomb blasts all around it. The training ship *Utah* was hit and capsized, taking fifty-eight men with her to the bottom of the harbor.

At approximately 8:10 A.M., a 1,700-pound (770-kilogram) bomb sliced through the deck of the battleship *Arizona*. The hit was so destructive that—in only nine minutes—the *Arizona* sank with 1,177 of her crew. That was the greatest loss of life on any ship and almost half the total number of Americans killed that day.

**The *Oklahoma* Goes Down**

"The thing that really sticks in my mind was the *Oklahoma* beginning to roll. She had a big explosion, and a hatch came off and went up in the air. . . . We had been told all our lives that you couldn't sink a battleship, and then to see one go upside down . . . it's heartbreaking. I knew how many were on the ship. I had a lot of shipmates there . . . and I knew they had gone down inside."

*Gunner's Mate Third Class George Waller, who was on the battleship* Maryland *anchored next to the* Oklahoma

When a huge bomb hit the *Arizona*, it ignited ammunition on board. This set off a tremendous explosion that sent a smoky fireball soaring high above the ship.

Sailors try to escape the sinking *California*, one of the first battleships to be hit in the attack. But the waters around them could be just as dangerous because of burning oil.

Within a few minutes, the tranquil harbor had become a fiery, blazing inferno. Dense clouds of black, oily smoke rose angrily into the blue Hawaiian sky. Oil that spilled out of the damaged ships quickly ignited, creating walls of flame on the open sea. Sailors who jumped into the water from sinking ships to escape death were burned horribly by the flaming oil.

## Other Targets

Although Pearl Harbor was the main target, Japanese planes struck other military sites on Oahu. They attacked Ford Island Naval Air Station, army airfields at Hickam, Wheeler, and Bellows, Ewa Marine Corps Air Station, Kaneohe Bay Naval Air Station, and Schofield Barracks. Kaneohe, located on Oahu's northern coast, was actually the first site attacked. The first bombs fell there at 7:48 A.M.

## A Hero in a Sinking Ship

Many sailors drowned because they were trapped below decks when ships sank. After being hit by six torpedoes, the *Oklahoma* "turned turtle"—navy slang for rolling over—and four hundred sailors died. Ensign Adolph Mortensen was trapped with three others in the ship's dispensary, which filled up almost completely with water. The four sailors located a porthole through which they could escape. One of them, Chief Carpenter Arnold Austin, was too big to get through the porthole, so he held it open for the others. "As far as I can tell," Mortensen said afterward, "I was the last man to escape from the ship without [outside] help. [Austin's] was the most noble and heroic act a man could perform, knowing full well that his minutes were few."

One of the Japanese planes flies over Pearl Harbor during the attack.

A fireball rises above one of the airfields attacked at Pearl Harbor. The airplanes were mostly laid out in rows on the airfields, vulnerable to attack from the air.

The goal in the airfield attacks was to destroy U.S. planes, which were easy targets that day. When General Short received the war warning on November 27, his main fear had been that enemy agents would try to **sabotage** U.S. aircraft. So that they could be watched, he ordered planes to be stored in neat lines, wing-tip to wing-tip, in the center of each base. Unfortunately, on December 7, this made it all the easier for the Japanese to destroy them. The attacking planes also fired their machine guns and killed many men racing around on the airfields below them.

About 8:35 A.M., the first wave of Japanese planes—their bombs and bullets exhausted—ended their attack. Within twenty minutes, the second wave arrived. These planes concentrated on finishing the destruction that the first group had begun. In the second phase of the attack, the ships *Shaw* and *Sotoyomo* were destroyed and the *Nevada* was heavily damaged. The planes also continued to hammer Hickam and Kaneohe air bases.

Shortly before 10 A.M., the last Japanese planes flew back to their carriers. The attack was finally over.

## Response on the Ground

Confusion reigned when the attack began, and the enemy planes were at first mistaken for American aircraft. When the first bombs hit Ford Island, Navy radio operator Harry R. Mead thought they were U.S. planes practicing. He wondered, "What is going on? Those dummies are using live ammunition."

The planes were finally identified as Japanese by the red circles painted on their tails and wing tips—Japan's symbol as the "Land of the Rising Sun." Lieutenant Commander Logan Ramsey then radioed to the world the first warning of the attack: "AIR RAID PEARL HARBOR. THIS IS NOT DRILL."

As the bombs fell, sailors on board ship and soldiers and airmen on land valiantly tried to defend themselves. They rushed to their battle stations and began firing machine guns and antiaircraft guns. Some of the enemy planes flew low to the ground. At Hickam Field, Machinist Mate Leon Bennett remembered, "You could see them grinning. They were laughing." Some pilots even waved at the men they were trying to kill.

## Fighting Back

Only fourteen U.S. pilots managed to get into the air. One was Lieutenant Kenneth Taylor, who was refueling his P-40 fighter at Wheeler Field. Taylor never hesitated when the attack began. "I just simply gave the P-40 the throttle and headed directly into the attacking airplanes," Taylor said. "I was able to start getting hits on them, shooting at them even before my wheels left the ground."

Men at Pearl Harbor take up defense positions to man the anti-aircraft guns on Ford Island. In the background is the *Nevada*, whose crew made a brave attempt to fight back.

Taylor shot down four enemy planes. Other pilots shot down seven more before fighting ended.

The bravery of the soldiers and sailors who fought back at Pearl Harbor was honored by the medals they won. The awards given to participants include 15 Medals of Honor, 51 Navy Crosses, and 69 Silver Stars.

One effort to fight back was made by the battleship *Nevada*, already badly damaged, which attempted to leave the harbor so it could fight more effectively. But when the *Nevada* tried to break away at about 8:50 A.M., enemy planes massed to attack it. "The Japanese bombers swarmed down on us like bees," said Lieutenant

## Dorie Miller (1919—1943)

One of the men who fought back was sailor Doris (Dorie) Miller, a twenty-two-year-old from Waco, Texas, who was a cook's assistant and star boxer on the USS *West Virginia*. When the attack began, Miller helped move wounded personnel to safety. He then manned a machine gun, even though he had not been trained to fire it. "It wasn't hard," Miller said, "I just pulled the trigger and she worked fine. I had watched the others with these guns. I guess I fired her for about fifteen minutes. I think I got one of those Jap planes. They were diving pretty close to us." He kept firing until heat and flames from the burning ship forced him to leap into the ocean along with other sailors. Miller received the Navy Cross for his heroism, becoming the first African American to receive the award. He died on Thanksgiving Day 1943 when his new ship, the USS *Liscome Bay*, sank during a battle.

The Navy Cross

Lawrence Ruff. After being hit several more times, the *Nevada*, fearing it would be sunk and block the harbor entrance, grounded itself on Hospital Point. While the *Nevada* was underway, however, the actions of its crew drew the cheers of sailors watching from other ships.

## Confusion in Battle

A battlefield is often a confusing place. Sometimes, combatants do not even know who they are shooting at. This happened at Pearl Harbor.

Not long after the attack began, the eleven B-17s that had been expected to fly in from California finally arrived. About the same time, a squadron of fourteen scout bombers from the *Enterprise*, an aircraft carrier that had been away from port, also tried to land. Both groups of planes were shot at by their countrymen.

"Don't shoot, this is an American plane," one pilot radioed. All but one of the B-17s were able to land safely, including one that set down on a golf course. But seven of the planes from the *Enterprise* were shot down and several airmen died.

One of the B-17s that arrived from California during the attack on Pearl Harbor lies wrecked and burning at Hickam airfield.

# After the Attack

In the foreground, rescuers approach the burning and sinking battleship *West Virginia*, hoping to help survivors.

## The Casualties

Pearl Harbor was the greatest disaster in U.S. naval history. There were 21 ships sunk or damaged, including 8 battleships, while 164 planes were destroyed and 159 damaged. Only 29 enemy aircraft were shot down, but 5 midget submarines were captured.

The human loss was much more terrible. That day, 2,340 soldiers and sailors were killed and 1,143 wounded. The Japanese losses were minimal: 55 airmen and 9 of the 10 sailors in the midget submarines. The tenth submarine occupant became the first prisoner of war captured by the United States. As for civilians in Hawaii, 68 died and 35 were injured.

The attack on Pearl Harbor had taken less than two hours. The job of tending the wounded, burying the dead, and repairing the damage would last far longer.

## Helping the Injured

The most immediate need was caring for the injured sailors and soldiers who had been shot, wounded in explosions, or burned by fire after jumping out of their ships into the deadly flames of the harbor.

Some of the injured swam ashore, many to Ford Island, while rescuers in small boats hauled other victims to safety. Medical facilities quickly filled to overflowing, and the wounded were placed wherever there was room. Ted LeBaron, stationed at the Naval Air Station, remembers that when he entered the Ford Island dining hall for something to eat after he spent hours helping wounded sailors, "Every single table had a man or a [dead] body stretched out on it."

Some of the wounded were civilians in Honolulu, which lay just a few miles east of Pearl Harbor. Some Japanese bombs fell there, but Honolulu was also struck by shells fired by U.S. forces that missed their targets—the Japanese planes—and carried on into the city.

This car, 8 miles (13 km) from Pearl Harbor, was hit by shrapnel during the attack. The driver, still in his seat, died along with two other victims.

## Rescue Efforts

Rescuers desperately tried to save sailors trapped in overturned ships. Workers with torches and drills cut open steel hulls, managing to free many men. Rescuers often knew where the trapped men were because they could hear them tapping on the hulls or shouting for help. This tense, furious rescue operation went on for days and saved scores of lives. Twenty-four men were rescued on December 8 from the *Oklahoma* alone.

## Caring for the Dead

There were also the dead to care for. Their bodies had to be identified and prepared for burial. Father Marcus Valenta spent many hours giving last rites, a Roman Catholic blessing for the dead, who were everywhere about him. "They had boys lying out on the lawn in front of a little first-aid station," Father Valenta remembered.

Soldiers and sailors pay their respects beside the mass grave of fifteen of the men who were killed in the bombing of Pearl Harbor.

Salvage workers survey the wreck of the battleship *Oklahoma*. Many men lost their lives trapped inside this ship, but others were saved by those who worked day and night to rescue them.

## Repairing the Ships

After saving lives, the next most important task following the attack on Pearl Harbor was to salvage as many of the damaged ships as possible. The survivors knew the vessels would be needed to help defeat Japan. And luckily for the United States, the Japanese planes had not heavily damaged Pearl Harbor's excellent repair facilities.

By the end of February 1942, navy personnel and others had repaired the battleships *Pennsylvania*, *Maryland*, and *Tennessee*, the cruisers *Honolulu*, *Helena*, and *Raleigh*, and the destroyers *Helm* and *Shaw*. Some were ready for active service; others were made seaworthy enough to sail to California for further repairs.

### Searching Among the Dead

"I would run along the aisle [of dead and wounded bodies] and, knowing my brother's characteristics, look for him. He chewed his nails. I knew where he had a wart. I'd say, 'Well, this guy looks like him,' but I couldn't see his face. I'd pick up a hand, and I'd say, 'No, that's not him, and then go on.'"

*Seaman Nick L. Kouretas of the* Raleigh *explaining how he searched for his brother, whom he finally found alive*

## Below the Surface

Re-floating ships that had sunk was more of a challenge. But within six months, repair crews enabled the battleships *Nevada*, *California*, and *West Virginia* to return to action. One of the hardest jobs was repairing sections of damaged ships that were underwater. Navy and civilian divers made approximately five thousand dives to accomplish this exhausting work.

The saddest part of salvage work was discovering bodies of sailors who had died. When salvage workers were repairing the *West Virginia*, they found chalk marks that showed some of the twenty sailors in one compartment of the ship had survived for seventeen days, until December 24.

Some ships were beyond repair. The destroyer *Downes* (left) supports the remains of the destroyer *Cassin* (right) in a dock at Pearl Harbor.

## Uniting a Nation

The tragedy of Pearl Harbor united the nation as never before behind a single cause: to defeat Japan. Even the leading isolationist, Senator Wheeler, declared after the attack, "The only thing now to do is to lick the hell out of them."

## A Declaration of War

On December 8, President Roosevelt asked Congress to declare war against Japan. The declaration meant that the United States would also have to fight Germany and Italy, Japan's Axis partners. Defeating those powerful nations would be a difficult task, but Roosevelt believed the United States could do it. He ended his request to Congress by declaring: "With confidence in our armed forces—with the unbounding determination of our people—we will gain the inevitable triumph—so help us God."

## Remember Pearl Harbor

The December 9 edition of the *Oregonian*, a Portland, Oregon, newspaper, coined a phrase that would be one of World War II's most famous: "Remember Pearl Harbor." Those simple words became part of the driving force that led the United States to victory, inspiring soldiers and civilians alike. The phrase, which also became the title of a popular song, was similar to the war cry, "Remember the Alamo!" that Texans voiced during their 1836 fight for independence from Mexico. "Remember Pearl Harbor" became a reminder to honor Americans who died at Pearl Harbor.

As the United States entered World War II, posters, such as the one below, encouraged citizens and members of the military in their war effort.

The Senate voted unanimously, 82-0, to declare war against Japan. The House of Representatives, vote, however, was 388-1. The single "no" vote in Congress was a vote for nonviolence, cast by Representative Jeannette Rankin, a **pacifist** from Montana. She had also voted in 1917 against entering World War I.

The American effort in World War II would be a massive one. Before Pearl Harbor, the U.S. military had only 1,670,000 men and women in uniform. By 1945, this figure climbed to more than 7,000,000. The war also demanded tremendous hard work and many sacrifices by civilians, who produced the planes, guns, and other weapons that the American war effort required.

...*we here highly resolve that these dead shall not have died in vain*...

*REMEMBER DEC. 7th!*

# The United States in World War II

After its attack on Pearl Harbor, Japan moved on to conquer great areas of the Pacific. This map shows the extent of Japanese control by 1942, at which time the Allies began to fight back.

### The Japanese Offensive

Admiral Isoroku Yamamoto had successfully attacked Pearl Harbor, but he was worried that the United States would still be strong enough to defeat Japan. "I fear," the admiral said, "we have only awakened a sleeping giant and filled him with terrible resolve."

Yamamoto was right: American might had awoken with a jolt from its isolationist slumber, and the nation was ready to go to war. The United States faced a huge task, however, because the attack on Pearl Harbor was just the start of a mighty Japanese **offensive** across the South Pacific. In just a few months, the Japanese overcame U.S. forces in the Philippines and on islands such as Guam and Midway. They also defeated the British in Singapore and Hong Kong and overran Burma and other nations in the Far East.

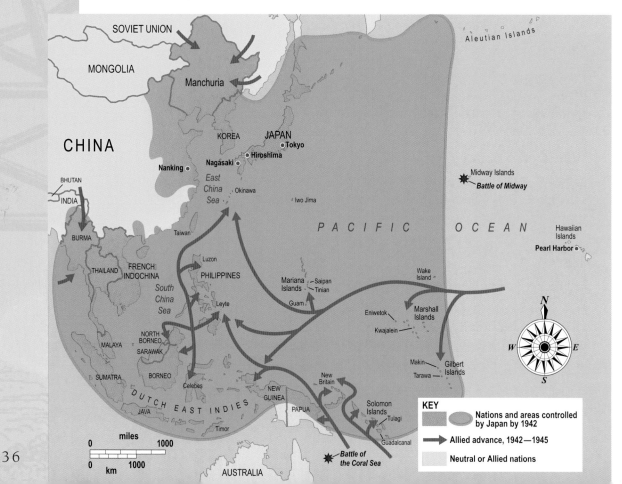

Colonel James Doolittle (fourth from right) and his pilots pose for a photograph in China after the Doolittle Raid of April 1942. The raid on four Japanese cities was a boost to the morale of Americans as the United States entered World War II.

## The United States Responds

The U.S. response to Pearl Harbor took a few months. On April 18, 1942, the United States struck its first blow against Japan. On that day, sixteen B-25 bombers took off from the aircraft carrier *Hornet*, which had sailed to within 650 miles (1,045 km) of Japan. Led by Lieutenant Colonel James Doolittle, the planes bombed Tokyo and other cities. The raid did little damage, but it greatly boosted American morale.

The Pearl Harbor attack weakened the Pacific Fleet, but it had failed to destroy the heart of U.S. naval power. The fleet's six aircraft carriers had been out at sea during the attack and so they were undamaged. In the summer of 1942, just months after the attack on Pearl Harbor, these carriers played a huge part in helping the United States win the Battle of the Coral Sea and the Battle of Midway. The two victories stopped the Japanese, who were nearing Australia, from continuing to capture more territory. From then until the end of the war, the Japanese were on the defensive as the United States and its allies continued to attack them.

**A Popular Song**
"Let's REMEMBER PEARL HARBOR, as we go to meet the foe. Let's REMEMBER PEARL HARBOR, as we did the Alamo. We will always remember, how they died for liberty. Let's REMEMBER PEARL HARBOR, and go on to victory. "

*Lyrics to one of World War II's most popular songs, "Remember Pearl Harbor," written by Don Reid and Sammy Kaye*

## Rising from the Ashes

After the attack, Pearl Harbor was a smoking, fiery ruin. During World War II, however, this military installation became bigger and more important than ever. As the headquarters for U.S. armed forces during the war against Japan in the Pacific, Pearl Harbor was vital to the war effort.

## The Atomic Bomb

Over the next three years, the Allies continued to fight World War II in Europe and the Pacific. After Germany surrendered in May 1945, the Allies turned their attention to Japan. By then, the United States had a new president, Harry S. Truman. Truman had just succeeded Franklin D. Roosevelt, who died in April. The United States also had a new weapon capable of winning the war: the atomic bomb.

On board the USS *Missouri*, General Hsu Yungchang of Japan signs the surrender document on September 2, 1945. After the surrender, the Allies—mostly U.S. troops—occupied Japan until 1952.

A conflict that began with the bombing of Pearl Harbor ended with devastating nuclear attacks on two Japanese cities. On August 6, 1945, a B-29 dropped an atomic bomb on Hiroshima, killing about eighty thousand people. When Japan refused to surrender after the first nuclear attack in history, Truman ordered a second atomic bomb dropped on Nagasaki. The second bomb, on August 9, killed more than forty thousand people and made the Japanese realize it was hopeless to continue fighting the Allies.

On August 14, 1945, Japan surrendered and World War II was over. Victory, however, had come at a high cost. In nearly four years of fighting in World War II, about 300,000 U.S. military personnel were killed and around 700,000 were wounded.

### Using the Bomb

"Having found the bomb we have used it. We have used it against those who attacked us without warning at Pearl Harbor. We have used it in order to shorten the agony of war, in order to save the lives of thousands and thousands of young Americans. We shall continue to use it until we completely destroy Japan's power to make war. Only a Japanese surrender will stop us."

*President Harry S. Truman explaining why he decided to use the atomic bomb on Japan*

World War II caused a wave of 6 million women to move into the workplace to replace men who were in military service overseas. Defense factories, such as this one making parts for airplanes, employed women in jobs traditionally held by men.

## Effects of the War at Home

World War II forever changed the lives of the soldiers and sailors who had to fight in far-off lands. But the war also created many significant changes at home. The massive war spending created millions of jobs for Americans who manufactured ships, planes, and weapons to win the war. The booming new economy ended the financial suffering of the Great Depression.

The war led to massive shifts in population as men and women moved around the nation to take new jobs at defense plants. By the end of 1945, more than 15 million civilians were living in a different county than they had lived in before Pearl Harbor. The shift in population included more than 700,000 African Americans, who moved from the South to California and big cities in the North to find good jobs. This huge migration had a dramatic impact on the racial makeup of many large cities.

The Hirano family, interned at the Colorado River Relocation Center, displays a picture of a family member who has joined the military to fight in World War II. Many of the people interned during World War II were U.S. citizens; of those, two-thirds were actually born in the United States.

## Japanese Americans

Other people who relocated during the war were Japanese Americans. But theirs was a forced move, not a voluntary one. In 1942, the U.S. government forced 110,000 Japanese Americans to move to prison camps, believing they would take Japan's side during the conflict. This happened on the mainland but not in Hawaii, where there were so many Japanese Americans that they were accepted as a natural part of the population. The **internment** was a great injustice because Japanese Americans remained loyal to the United States and thousands fought for their country.

## Daniel Inouye (born 1924)

Daniel Inouye was a high school senior at McKinley High School in Honolulu during the attack on Pearl Harbor. When he saw the bombs start falling, he began screaming at the planes even though he himself was of Japanese descent. Inouye was angry because he feared, correctly, that a war with Japan would result in a backlash against his people. When the United States entered World War II, Inouye enlisted in the army and fought in Europe. He lost an arm in battle and won the Medal of Honor. After the war, Inouye went into politics. In 1962, he was elected as a U.S. senator, a post he held for more than four decades.

# Conclusion

There are still people alive today who were present during the attack on Pearl Harbor. These men were all serving in the U.S. Army or Navy at Pearl Harbor when it was attacked in 1941. They returned to Hawaii in December 2001 for the sixtieth anniversary of the bombing.

## Why Was Pearl Harbor Unprepared?

After Pearl Harbor, Americans were shocked that U.S. forces had been so unready for the surprise attack. Initial investigations by Congress and the military blamed the commanders in Hawaii, Admiral Kimmel and General Short. Official reports stated that Kimmel and Short had failed to protect their men, and both officers were relieved of their commands.

In later years, however, new evidence has shown that many people besides Kimmel and Short were at fault. In 1995, a report by the U.S. Defense Department concluded that the blame for being unprepared "should be broadly shared" by many military and civilian leaders. It claimed "the run-up to Pearl Harbor was fraught with miscommunication, oversights, and lack of follow-up." The report noted that officials in Washington failed to keep Kimmel and Short informed of many developments concerning Japan. The worst oversight was the failure on December 7 to deliver the final warning before the attack itself began.

## Pearl Harbor Today

Pearl Harbor—now officially known as Navy Region Hawaii—has remained an important military installation. Today it is a sprawling

The 184-foot-(56-meter-) long memorial rests across the deck of the still sunken *Arizona*. Visitors, more than 1.5 million people a year, are ferried by navy personnel to the memorial.

complex spread over thousands of acres of land and water. Home to well over eighty thousand members of the military and their families, Pearl Harbor is like a small city with its housing, churches, stores, and schools.

More than six decades after the USS *Arizona* sank, drops of oil still escape from its shattered remains and float to the surface. The rusted skeleton of the once mighty battleship lies beneath a stark white shrine, a building that was dedicated on Memorial Day in 1962. The memorial honors all those who were killed December 7, 1941, but especially the 1,177 sailors who died aboard the *Arizona*.

## The Legacy of Pearl Harbor

The *Arizona* Memorial is seen by some as a monument to American history and by others as a memorial to the men who died in battle. But the memorial also represents a far-reaching legacy that arose out of the attack on Pearl Harbor. The anger, grief, and hatred they felt forced Americans to end their isolationism and take an active part in world affairs. In order to survive in the future, the United States would have to continue to ally itself with other nations.

# Time Line

| | |
|---|---|
| **1887** | United States acquires exclusive right to Pearl Harbor. |
| **1893** | January 16: Hawaiian monarch Queen Lili'uokalani is overthrown by Americans. |
| **1898** | July 7: President William McKinley signs bill annexing Hawaii as a U.S. territory. |
| **1937** | Japan invades China. |
| **1939** | September 1: German troops invade Poland to begin World War II in Europe. |
| **1940** | May: Pearl Harbor becomes headquarters of U.S. Navy's Pacific Fleet. |
| | September: Japan, Germany, and Italy sign Tripartite Pact. |
| | September 16: President Franklin Delano Roosevelt signs the Selective Service Training and Service Act to create first peacetime draft. |
| | November 7: Roosevelt is reelected as president. |
| **1941** | March: Congress passes Lend-Lease Act, which provides supplies to nations fighting Axis Powers. |
| | July 25: Roosevelt bans shipments of scrap iron and gasoline to Japan and freezes all Japanese assets in the United States. |
| | December 7: Japan attacks Pearl Harbor. |
| | December 8: The United States declares war on Japan. |
| **1942** | February: Roosevelt signs order to intern Japanese Americans. |
| | April 18: Bombers from the aircraft carrier USS *Hornet* bomb Tokyo and other Japanese cities. |
| | May 4–8: Battle of the Coral Sea. |
| | June 4–6: Battle of Midway. |
| **1945** | April 12: Roosevelt dies and Harry S. Truman becomes president. |
| | May 7: Germany surrenders to Allies. |
| | August 6: United States drops atomic bomb on Hiroshima, Japan. |
| | August 9: United States drops atomic bomb on Nagasaki, Japan. |
| | August 14: Japan surrenders to Allies, ending World War II. |
| **1962** | Memorial Day: Memorial is dedicated on USS *Arizona* in Pearl Harbor. |

# Glossary

**aircraft carrier:** large ship with a long, flat deck on which planes can take off and land.

**allies:** people, groups or countries that agree to support and defend each other. Allies was also the name for the United States, Canada, and other nations fighting on the same side in World Wars I and II.

**amphibious:** adapted for land and water.

**annex:** take control of a country or region and make it officially part of another nation.

**assets:** property, money, investments, and other things of value.

**civilian:** person who is not serving in the armed forces.

**democratic:** based on a government system in which people vote on decisions or elect representatives to vote for them.

**deployment:** positioning of military forces and equipment.

**diplomat:** person who represents his or her country in another country.

**draft:** government system requiring people to serve in the armed forces if called upon.

**economy:** system of producing and distributing goods and services.

**fleet:** group of ships under a single command. In World War II, the Pacific Fleet was the U.S. Navy's entire naval force in and around the Pacific Ocean.

**infamy:** fame of a bad kind, such as that of a terrible event or person.

**intelligence:** information about enemies or enemy actions. Intelligence officers are people who find out as much as they can about possible enemies and their actions.

**internment:** imprisonment of people who have not been found guilty of any crime.

**interventionist:** person who gets involved or interferes in something. In World War II, it meant a person who believed the United States should help defend nations attacked by fascist nations.

**lease:** agreement to use property of another person. Usually, one person leases property to another person in exchange for money. Under the Lend-Lease Act, the United States lent ships, planes and weapons to Britain in exchange for a lease on British territory.

**minelayer:** ship that lays explosives underwater.

**navigable:** deep and wide enough for ships to pass through.

**neutrality:** position of taking neither side in a conflict.

**offensive:** large, planned attack.

**pacifist:** person who is against fighting for any reason, even if he or she is attacked.

**policy:** plan or way of doing things that is decided upon and then used in managing situations and making decisions.

**radar:** system using radio waves to detect and locate objects.

**sabotage:** destroy or damage something belonging to an enemy.

**torpedo:** missile launched through water to explode against a ship's hull.

**United States Territory:** geographical area that belongs to and is governed by the United States but is not included in any of its states.

# Further Information

## Books

Allen, Thomas B. and Robert D. Ballard. *Remember Pearl Harbor: American and Japanese Survivors Tell Their Stories*. National Geographic Society, 2001.

Denenberg, Barry. *Early Sunday Morning: The Pearl Harbor Diary of Amber Billows, Hawaii, 1941* (Dear America). Scholastic, 2001.

Spies, Karen Bornemann. *Franklin D. Roosevelt* (United States Presidents). Enslow, 1999.

Stanley, Jerry. *I Am an American: A True Story of Japanese Internment*. Crown, 1996.

Steins, Richard. *The Allies Against the Axis: World War II (1940–1950)*. Twenty First Century Books, 1995.

## Web Sites

**www.arizonamemorial.org/pearlharbor** Good information and pictures presented by the *Arizona* Memorial Museum Association, dedicated to the history of the attack on Pearl Harbor.

**www.nps.gov/usar** Web site of the National Park Service that runs the *Arizona* Memorial in Pearl Harbor.

**plasma.nationalgeographic.com/pearlharbor/** National Geographic web site is full of information, pictures, and animated material relating to Pearl Harbor.

## Useful Addresses

**USS *Arizona* Memorial**
National Park Service
1 Arizona Memorial Place
Honolulu, HI 96818
Telephone: (808) 422-0561

# Index

Page numbers in *italics* indicate maps and diagrams. Page numbers in **bold** indicate other illustrations.